An IT Manager's Guide to Hardware Asset Management

Laurence E Tindall

An IT Manager's Guide to Hardware Asset Management

Copyright © 2018 Laurence Tindall

ISBN: 9781729316900

Printed in the United States of America

First Edition

Original illustrations by Laurence Tindall

Dedication

To my wife, mum, and dad, thank you for always pushing me to work hard. I dedicate this book to you.

About the Author

Laurence Tindall is an IT professional from
the United Kingdom and currently resides in
Colorado. Laurence is a seasoned IT Asset
Management guru who loves every aspect
of ITAM, and is an advocate on the subject.
Laurence has spent several years working
in the IT industry and has helped several organizations set up
their ITAM programs. Laurence enjoys organizing companies'
IT assets, and saving money through the management of
them.

Laurence is currently a Product Manager for an IT Asset
Management company developing Products that assist
Fortune 500 companies manage their IT assets. When
Laurence isn't attending sprint planning sessions, or
prioritizing features, he enjoys the wonderful Colorado
outdoors, and traveling the world.

Before working in IT, Laurence studied Music Technology at
Kingston College, London, and Film Production at South
Thames College, London. After graduating college, Laurence
shifted gears from the media industry to focus on a career in
Information Technology.

Table of Contents

Introduction

Have you ever wondered about that shiny barcode on your laptop at work? Or why the IT Engineer scans your device before working on your computer? That is all part of IT Asset Management (ITAM). IT Asset Management ensures all assets are tracked and accounted for in an organization to ensure the maximum value is returned from each asset, and all assets are safe and secure at all times.

In this book, you will learn about what IT Asset Management is, and how it can benefit an organization, it also provides the essentials to setup up an IT Asset Management program from the ground up. This book is aimed towards all IT professionals, both new and experienced, that seek to challenge themselves in their knowledge and skills in IT Hardware Asset Management.

What is IT Asset Management (ITAM)

IT Asset Management (ITAM) is a set of business practices implemented by an organization to track its hardware and software assets. IT Asset Management joins inventory, financial, and contractual functions into one business practice. As Hardware Assets are the backbone of an organization and support its services, accurate tracking, management, and accountability is paramount.

Since technology is changing every day, the need for IT Asset Management is ever growing. As the technology industry is ever changing, the refresh cycle of assets is becoming more and more frequent. This applies direct pressure onto businesses to ensure all IT investments are tracked and accounted for at all times. With the introduction of the **General Data Protection Regulation (GDPR)**, more businesses than ever before are seeing the need to track all of their IT assets and software to protect their business and reputation.

Hardware Asset Management (HAM) ensures the financial cost of each asset is tracked to help businesses make systematic purchasing decisions when it comes to the refresh of assets. Hardware Asset Management also involves managing; warranties, contracts, vendor agreements, and software licenses.

Without Asset Management, organizations wouldn't know:

- What assets they own
- Where they are located
- Who is using them
- How much value is gained from them
- How they support the business
- What potential risks they pose
- What information is on them

One of the most fundamental goals of IT Asset Management is to ensure the maximum value is gained from every asset purchased.

Examples of Assets

Hardware assets include devices such as; computers, laptops, servers, network switches, monitors, printers, mobile phones, IP phones, hard drives, routers, and firewalls to name a few. Hardware Assets are known as **Tangible Assets** because they are physical and can be touched.

Intangible Assets are assets that cannot be seen or touched. Assets such as software, license agreements, and contract agreements are examples of intangible assets because they are non-physical and invisible.

Tangible Assets	Intangible Assets
Physical	Non-physical
Visible	Invisible
Holds a salvage value	Can Lose All Value
Easy to track	Difficult to track

Role of IT Asset Management within an Organization

The role of IT Asset Management within an organization is to manage and govern the end to end asset life-cycle, from the time an asset is purchased, all the way to when an asset is disposed. The Asset Management team is the point of contact for inquires such as;

- What assets are available in stock
- What assets belong to the organization
- Where are the assets located
- What systems do the assets support

More importantly, the IT Asset Management program ensure the maximum Return on Investment (ROI) is realized from every asset.

IT Asset Management regularly functions alongside Financial, Legal, Project Management Office (PMO), IT Governance, Security, and the IT Help Desk, as they all play a distinct role in the asset life-cycle.

Starting up an Asset Management Program

Starting an Asset Management program in an organization can take a lot of time and effort, but the outcomes and benefits will significantly benefit an organization in many aspects. A finely tuned asset management program can free up budgets, establish trust between IT and Finance, and make planning and forecasting as simple as clicking a button.

To start an Asset Management program in an organization requires Executive Buy In. Without executive buy in, it is unlikely to get resourcing or a budget to fund the program.

What is Executive Buy In?

Executive Buy In is when an executive level member of an organization fully supports a project. Supporting a project means that the executive will secure a budget, support the project, provide communication to other C-level executives, and generally combat any battles that may arise.

Executive Buy In is crucial for the overall success of a new project/initiative. In most organizations, it is the Chief Information Officer (CIO), or Chief Technology Officer (CTO) who supports and sponsors an IT Asset Management initiative.

Deciding what assets are In Scope vs Out of Scope

When starting up an Asset Management program, it will quickly become apparent that tracking every single asset is an overkill. That's why organizations will make a decision on which assets should be tracked vs not tracked. Weighing out the associated costs and benefits to track certain types of assets is the first step to determine whether or not an asset should be tracked. For example, would it make sense to track a USB cable, what would the benefits be, and what would the financial implications be if that USB cable was lost?

When tracking assets, be sure to factor in the manpower costs associated with tracking the asset. If something is of low financial value and does not pose a security risk, it may not make sense to track it. These decisions are made by organizations depending on their financial situation, and asset management support.

Here are a set of questions to ask yourself when deciding which types of assets should be tracked:

- Does the asset have the ability to store data?
- Does the asset cost more than $300?

- If the asset was lost, would it have a negative impact on the operation of the business?
- Is the asset difficult to replace?

By asking such questions, you will start to get a clear understanding of which assets should be tracked, vs not tracked. If you answered yes to any of the above questions, then it's recommended to track that type of asset.

It is not unusual for organizations to track every single asset, regardless of cost or type. This is due to strict security and data privacy policies put in place, which forces organizations to track absolutely everything.

Below is a table displaying different types of assets with the above questions answered:

Asset Type	Ability to store data?	Cost more than $300?	Hard to replace?	Should you track it?
Laptop	Yes	Yes	No	Yes
USB Flash Drive	Yes	No	No	Yes
VGA Cable	No	No	No	No
Keyboard	No	No	No	No
Server	Yes	Yes	No	Yes
Hardware VPN Token	No	No	Yes	Yes

Once management and leadership have decided which types of assets should be tracked, the next step is to clearly document which assets will be tracked, and to ensure this information is readily available to all teams involved, in a process known as **Asset Categorization**.

Asset Categorization

In order to easily identify assets, it's recommended to create an end-to-end list of all asset categories in the organization.

Once there is a complete list of all asset categories, import the list into your asset repository, and assign each product to a defined category. This will help in the future with reporting, metrics, and asset requests from the IT Help Desk.

With a defined list of asset categories implemented, you will easily be able to answer enquiries such as:

- How many computers are in-stock?
- How many hard drives were disposed in the last year? Or
- How many mobile phones are in-use globally?

Sub-categories should be established when there is a wide variety of similar asset types, and the organization needs to run specific reports on certain types of assets.

Asset Category	Asset Class
Server	Hardware
Computer	Hardware
Mobile Phone	Hardware
External Hard Drive	Hardware
Software License	Software

Asset Repository

The asset repository is one of the most important tools that will be used in an Asset Management program. An **Asset Repository** is a software application that allows the Asset Management team to track the asset inventory accurately and precisely.

Asset Management repositories should have the ability to track the following asset data attributes:

- Serial Number
- Model Number
- Product SKU
- Asset tag
- Description
- Manufacturer
- Acquisition Method
- Cost and Currency
- Condition
- Category
- Managed By
- Installation Date
- Status
- Warranty Start and End Date
- Warranty Description
- Cost Center
- Disposal Date
- Disposal Vendor
- Asset Category
- Vendor
- Location
- Rack
- Rack Height (U)
- Owner
- Assigned to
- Contains Sensitive Data

Selecting an asset repository that has an email directory integration is really important.

This feature will ensure that when new employees start at the organization, their name, email address, and title will automatically be available in the asset repository system. This is extremely useful when assigning assets to employees.

The asset repository should also include a way for IT Asset Managers to flag assets that contain sensitive data. This feature can assist the security team in identifying and tracking high risk assets, and also helps when transporting and/or disposing assets.

When selecting an asset management repository system, make sure it includes features such as:

- Ability to process install, move, add, and delete changes to assets
- Service catalog for asset requests
- Purchase Order tracking
- Ability to log in-stock inventory
- Ability to run reports
- Export/Import features
- Notifications
- Mobile compatible
- Vendor management
- Contract management
- Check in/Check out features
- Asset Audit
- Maintenance Scheduling

Once you have selected an Asset Repository, you will need to import all of your asset data into the software. Most applications support the import of assets via an easy to use data importer.

Note: When searching for asset management repositories, ensure you look for applications that are hosted and maintained in the cloud by your software vendor. This will then transfer all maintenance, security, and platform support responsibilities to the vendor. This is crucial as you will require a system that is accessible 24x7, and most importantly, reliable. Software applications that fit into this model are typically classed as Software as a Service (SaaS) applications.

If you go down the route of hosting the application on premise, you will need to consider what will happen in the event of an outage, or a natural disaster.

Software as a Service (SaaS)

Software as a Service (SaaS) is a term commonly used in the IT industry that describes a software application that is hosted in the cloud by a software vendor. User access is gained to the application via the internet, enabling users to use the software anywhere, and at any time. Software as a Service (SaaS) applications are beneficial for organizations because it eliminates the need for internal servers to run the software on, as well as any related maintenance and upkeep.

Software as a Service (SaaS) applications are an attractive software model to organizations because they offer flexible pricing, little to no support costs, and hardware security responsibilities are shifted to the vendor.

Why Spreadsheets Don't Work

Over the years spreadsheets have become extremely useful for many different reasons, and have worked well for the functionalities they offer. In IT Asset Management, spreadsheets are not a good system of record for tracking assets and changes made to the inventory.

The following are just a few reasons why using spreadsheets to track assets is a bad practice:

- No history of changes
- No traceability or accountability
- No governance or audit trail
- 3rd party tool integrations are not possible
- Cannot handle large amounts of data
- Data can quickly become out-of-date and stale
- Error prone
- Notifications and alerts are not possible
- Version control can be problematic
- No access permissions or controls can be defined

Using an Asset Repository is important because it captures changes and enables multiple users to collaborate together. With a spreadsheet, only one user at a time can work on a file, so teamwork can be slow and unproductive. Spreadsheets are also error prone, meaning an IT Asset Manager can easily mistype a part number, or forget to enter a serial number when logging a new asset. Whereas an Asset Repository contains field validation that can prevent users from entering incorrect data.

An Asset Repository is also something that is updated in real-time, whereas a spreadsheet is a static document that has to be re-distributed to team members when changes are made.

While the initial cost of purchasing an Asset Repository is typically greater than a spreadsheet, the long term costs associated with maintaining a spreadsheet are far greater than an Asset Repository.

Making the decision to track assets in an Asset Repository in the early stages of an IT Asset Management initiative will make the implementation and management process a lot smoother.

Discovery Software

Discovery Software is a type of software that is installed in an organizations network that scans, discovers, and logs assets that are connected to it. Discovery Software can only detect assets that are Internet Protocol (IP) addressable. This means Discovery Software won't be able to discover devices that are not connected to the network. Take a set of speakers for example, because they are connected via an auxiliary port, and are not IP-addressable, they won't be detected when a scan is ran. This means that even when you have a discovery tool implemented, manual discovery and reconciliation efforts will still be required.

In IT Asset Management, Discovery Software plays a crucial role for the purpose of identifying changes, and relaying those changes back to the asset repository. Discovery Software also assists with the detection of new assets, identifying what software is on each device, and identifying rogue/unwanted devices. Most discovery tools log all changes that are made to each device, so if an asset moves, or leaves the network, each change is logged, and can be used to update the Asset Repository.

Using Discovery Software is a great way to obtain an accurate baseline of what assets are installed in a network. When starting an Asset Management program, it is best practice to use a discovery tool to harvest the initial asset baseline, as this data can be used as a good starting point to knowing what assets are already in a network.

Since discovery tools can identify the last time a device was turned on, or logged into, the IT Asset Management team can easily identify unused devices, and therefore save the organization IT costs. By monitoring and identifying unused assets, the IT Help Desk can collect unused assets, and return them to the Asset Management storeroom to be made available for redeployment. To make this procedure smooth, a policy should be created around unused devices. This will enable the IT Help Desk to collect and return unused assets.

Finding the right discovery tool with automation capabilities can greatly support the asset management team. A lot of discovery tools include integration functionalities, which allow automatic data updates to be made to your asset repository. These types of features significantly benefit the asset management team by reducing the amount of time in manually updating the asset repository.

Most Discovery Software applications have the ability to discover and log the following asset attributes:

- IP Address
- MAC Address

- Hostname
- Manufacturer
- Model Number
- Serial Number
- Location
- Memory
- Processor
- Storage Capacity
- Domain
- Operating System
- Install Date
- Last Seen on Network Date
- BIOS Version
- Software Installed

Agent Vs. Agentless

An agent based discovery tool is one that installs a tracking agent onto each device in the network. This allows the discovery software to always have access to a device whenever it's online, and allows it to access much greater depths of information.

Agent based discovery tools are beneficial in scenarios where assets frequently leave the network.

An agentless based discovery tool is one that doesn't install any tracking agents onto each device. Agentless Discovery can only access devices that are connected to the network. Agentless is commonly viewed as a non-intrusive method to discovery as it doesn't have administrative access to machines. Agentless is usually the preferred choice of discovery tool as it requires less overhead support, and is a lot easier to setup compared to agent based discovery tools.

Advantages of using Discovery Software

- Discovers the majority of IT hardware assets
- Can be integrated with the asset repository
- Is very cost effective
- Easily detects unwanted hardware/software
- Identifies which assets are being used vs unused

Disadvantages of using Discovery Software

- Not all assets are discovered
- Requires firewall configuration for scanning
- Opens up security risk
- Can be viewed as user intrusive

Responsibilities of an IT Asset Manager

When starting an IT Asset Management program, it can be tough trying to determine what responsibilities are in scope, vs out of scope. By having a documented list of responsibilities, all departments of an organization will easily understand what the responsibilities of the IT Asset Management team are.

In a typical IT Asset Management department, IT Asset Managers are responsible for fulfilling the following duties:

- Receiving assets
- Deploying assets to IT Engineers
- Applying asset tags to hardware assets
- Logging assets into the asset repository
- Logging Installs, Moves, Adds, Changes (IMACs)
- Logging warranties
- Logging purchase orders, and other contractual agreements
- Assisting with Request for Proposals (RFPs)
- Conducting random spot checks for inventory accuracy
- Ensuring the wellbeing of assets at all times
- Managing the asset repository
- Monitoring the Total Cost of Ownership (TCO) for all assets
- Processing Return Merchandize Authorizations (RMAs)
- Updating the Configuration Management Database (CMDB)

- Safely securing assets while in the custody of the ITAM team
- Processing asset disposal requests
- Responding to all asset related inquires
- Ensuring all storerooms have adequate amounts of assets in-stock
- Coordinating with Executives, IT Help Desk, IT Security, Finance, Procurement, and Project Management Office (PMO)

Depending on the maturity stage of an ITAM program, not all of the above duties may be in place.

Processes

Whether you are starting an Asset Management program, or enhancing an existing one, processes are always important to implement. Processes ensure employees on the Asset Management team know what to do and when. Processes are also good for identifying deficiencies in the way existing tasks are performed.

Here is a list of typical process documents that should be designed and implemented for any Asset Management program:

- **Asset Receiving Process** - this document includes who receives and validates newly purchased assets as they are delivered to the premises.
- **Asset Check Out Process** – this document covers how and when assets should be checked out and deployed to IT engineers.
- **Asset Check In Process** - this document covers the necessary steps to be taken when assets are being returned for storage.
- **Install, Move, Add, Change (IMAC) Process** - this document covers when and how the asset repository

should be updated when changes to the inventory occur.

- **Asset Audit Process** – this document comprises of how and when an asset audit should take place.
- **Asset Reconciliation Process** – this document covers when a reconciliation should take place, and who is responsible.
- **Lost or Stolen Asset Process** – this document covers the steps that need to be taken when an asset is either stolen or lost.
- **Employee Termination Process** – this document covers the return of assets when an employee is leaving a company.
- **Team RACI** – this document lists out every asset management function, and specifies who is responsible, accountable, consulted, and informed.
- **Asset Disposal Process** – this document covers how assets are safely and securely disposed.

Install, Move, Add, Change (IMAC)

Install, Move, Add, Change (IMAC) is the term used to describe when an asset's configuration is changed in its life-cycle.

An *install* is when a new asset is installed and configured into the network. A *move* is when an asset is relocated from one location to another. A *add* is when a new piece of hardware or software is added to an existing asset. A *change* is the modification to an existing asset, this could include going into maintenance or being decommissioned.

The following are some example scenarios demonstrating the different types of IMAC changes that could happen through the life-cycle of a server:

- **Install** - A new server is procured and installed in a data center.

- **Move** – The server is moved from the data center in Phoenix, AZ to the data center in Dallas, TX.
- **Add** – A larger hard-drive is added to the server to increase its storage capacity.
- **Change** – The server is decommissioned and moved to a storage facility due to its age and slowness.

When an IMAC occurs, it's important to update the Asset Repository with the changes made. This ensures that all asset data is kept 100% accurate and up to date. The IMAC process is designed to cover all possible configuration changes throughout an asset's lifecycle. The IMAC process is a framework setup to ensure all changes made to an assets configuration are identified and logged.

In most organizations, the IT Help Desk department are the people who initiate the majority of IMAC changes to an asset. This means that the IT Help Desk always need to be aligned with the IMAC process, and have access to the Asset Repository for the purpose of updating assets.

In most organizations, the IT Help Desk will use mobile devices to update the Asset Repository as IMAC changes are made. This allows IT Engineers to carry on with their main duties without having to remember what assets were moved or configured when returning to their workstation.

Return Merchandize Authorization (RMA)

When working in IT, you will most likely hear the term RMA frequently. **Return Merchandize Authorization (RMA)** is the process that happens when a faulty asset which is covered under a warranty or service contract, is then returned to the manufacturer or supplier to be repaired, replaced, or refunded.

In an organization, the Asset Management team and IT Help Desk are typically responsible for fulfilling the RMA process.

The RMA process begins when an asset is identified to be damaged, or not working as expected.

Steps to processing an RMA:

1. Contact the manufacturer to validate that the asset is covered under a warranty or support agreement. Ensure you have the following information available; Model Number, Serial Number, Coverage Information, and the issue identified with the asset.
2. Once you have contacted the manufacturer, and they have authorized the return of the asset, package up the asset for shipment. Most warranty providers will supply you with free shipping labels as part of the support agreement.
3. Ship the asset to the manufacturer, ensure you log the tracking number in the asset repository. This will help with tracking down the package if it gets lost or not delivered.
4. Once the manufacturer receives the faulty asset, they will either ship you a new one, repair the asset and return it, or issue a refund for the value of the asset.

Depending on the supplier or **Original Equipment Manufacturer (OEM)**, different RMA types can be performed. The following list contains the most common RMA types:

- **Advance Exchange**: When a manufacturer immediately ships out a new asset to you, to replace the existing faulty asset. The manufacturer doesn't wait for the return of the faulty asset.
- **Exchange**: When a manufacturer swaps your faulty asset with another one.
- **Credit**: When a manufacturer issues you a credit note upon the return of a faulty asset.
- **Refund**: The manufacturer issues you a cash refund for the cost of the asset.

The term RMA is sometimes referred to as **Return Authorization (RA)**, **Return to Vendor (RTV)**, and **Return Goods Authorization (RGA).** These terms are merely iterations for Return Merchandize Authorization (RMA) and all refer to the same process.

Tax Savings

Depending on the country or countries your organization is located in, the Finance department may be able to gain financially from tax deductions based upon the acquisition and/or depreciation of assets. Every country is different, so this may not apply to your organization. Tax savings can help reduce the overall spend in an organization. This is another example of why keeping an up-to-date and accurate asset repository is a key factor in the success of an asset management program.

The Asset Life-cycle

The asset lifecycle consists of 5 stages; planning, acquisition, deployment, management, and retirement & disposition.

Stage 1: Planning

The Planning stage of the asset life-cycle is the first and most important stage. In this stage, management will decide whether to purchase, lease, or even re-use existing assets to fulfill the organizational needs. Key stakeholders and decision makers will assess and understand how much value the introduction of new assets will bring to the organization. During the planning phase, key stakeholders will evaluate the following questions:

- What are the problems we are trying to solve by acquiring these assets?
- What is the Return on Investment (ROI) when introducing these assets?
- What maintenance will be required to maintain and support these assets?

- How much electrical energy will these new assets consume?
- Will these new assets increase productivity?
- Do we already own similar assets that can deliver the same outcome?

These types of questions will help management make informative decisions on whether new assets should be introduced into the organization.

Stage 2: Acquisition

The second stage of the asset life-cycle is the Acquisition stage. Acquiring assets is the stage when the procurement department go through the formal process to acquire new assets. Typically in most organizations, large asset purchases are processed through the RFI, RFP, and RFQ process. Shortly after a Purchase Order (PO) has been placed, assets are delivered to the organization. Generally, the acquisition stage includes the following major activities:

- Request for Information (RFI)
- Request for Proposal (RFP)
- Request for Quote (RFQ)
- Purchase Order (PO)
- Assets are shipped and delivered
- Assets are received, inspected, and placed into storage

Depending on the size of the purchase, not all assets enter an organization through the formal procurement process. Sometimes new assets are introduced into an organization through petty cash/employee funded purchases.

Stage 3: Deployment

The Deployment stage of the asset life-cycle is where newly purchased assets, or existing assets are deployed into operation. Assets are usually issued to end users via fulfillment requests that are generated and assigned to the IT Help Desk.

In most organizations, assets are deployed from the IT Asset Management storeroom. This is the location where IT Engineers go to collect assets that will be installed for operation.

The asset deployment stage includes the following activities:

- Request Fulfillment
- Asset Deployment (Check-out)

Stage 4: Management

The Management stage of the asset life-cycle is the lengthiest stage, and covers various activities. In this stage, assets are deployed for use in the organization. While the assets are in operation, the Asset Management team maintain the correctness of the data in the asset repository relating to all assets. This ensures the location and ownership of each asset is accounted for at all times.

The IT Help Desk and Technology teams support and maintain all assets while they are in-use, all the way through until an asset is deemed to no longer hold any functional value. Depending on the type of asset, some assets may be in operation for several months, whereas some can be in-use for many years.

The management stage typically includes activities such as:

- Upgrades
- Maintenance
- Installs, Moves, Adds, and Changes (IMACs)

Once an asset is deemed to hold no value for its particular purpose, it is then returned back to the IT Asset storeroom for storage. Once an asset is kept in storage, the IT and

Technology teams will regularly review the assets to determine if they can be redeployed.

Stage 5: Retirement & Disposition

The Retirement and Disposition stage is the final stage of the asset life-cycle. This stage covers the retirement and disposition of assets. This is when an asset reaches its end of life, and no longer provides any value to an organization.

Once an asset is identified to no longer hold any useful value to an organization, it is then processed through the IT Asset Disposition (ITAD) process. The ITAD process ensures all assets are safely, and securely removed from the organization. This process is heavily governed by the IT Security department to ensure all company data is destroyed or wiped before any assets can leave the premises.

Usually when IT assets are disposed, an IT Asset Disposition (ITAD) vendor will collect the assets and recycle and/or destroy them.

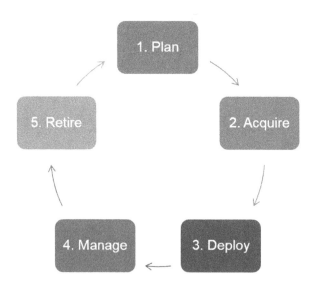

Asset Procurement

Asset Procurement is a term widely used across organizations and vendors which describes the coordination efforts used to purchase and acquire new assets for an organization.

As mentioned previously in this book, not every organization procure goods and services in the same way. In most organizations, issuing an RFI, RFP, and RFQ is a common practice when assets are being procured.

When a decision has been made to procure new assets, a **Purchase Requisition (PR)** request is typically made and submitted to the Procurement department. Purchase Requisition requests are usually created and submitted through an **Enterprise Resource Planning (ERP)** software application. Once a Purchase Requisition request has been made, the organization will most likely proceed with the RFI, RFP, and RFQ process.

Request for Information (RFI)

Once a Purchase Requisition has been approved by procurement, the next step is for finance to create a Request for Information (RFI) document.

Once the RFI document is created, it is then sent to a wide variety of vendors and is used for gathering information around the products and services each vendor has to offer. The RFI is also used to determine the suitability around the possible business opportunities with a vendor.

The RFI document also helps an organization gather information about vendors to determine which one may be the best fit. Typically in this process, the organization aims to create a list of preferred vendors. Once the RFI responses are received, they are kept for the next stage.

After the Procurement department is satisfied with the responses received from the RFI, the Procurement department will work on the Request for Proposal (RFP).

Request for Proposal (RFP)

A **Request for Proposal (RFP)** is a document that is sent out to existing or potential vendors for the purpose of procuring new assets or services. An RFP document is an invitation to vendors to participate in the selection process for a new business proposal.

An RFP document typically covers the following topics:

- Problems to be resolved
- RFP selection criteria
- Statement of purpose
- Payment terms
- Incentives (if any)
- Contractual Terms and Conditions
- Asset Requirements (Specifications, Configuration Requirements, preferred Manufacturers)
- Response deadlines
- Response methods
- Points of contact for questions
- Process schedule

It is important that the requirements within the RFP are specific. An example of a set of requirements in an asset RFP for the procurement of new computers could be:

- The Random Access Memory (RAM) should be a minimum of 16GB
- The hard-drive capacity should be a minimum of 500GB
- The processor should have a minimum clock speed of 3.2 GHz

Benefits of using an RFP in Asset Management

Using an RFP process to purchase assets are beneficial for
the following reasons:

- It allows you to compare prices across multiple
  vendors to ensure that you get the best price
  available.
- Demonstrates an equal and fair business selection
  process to all vendors and suppliers.
- Allows you to negotiate a lower price with other
  vendors.
- Keeps existing vendors up to date with market trends
  and demands.
- Opens new business opportunities for new vendors in
  the marketplace.
- Demonstrates to the Finance department that you are
  cost-centric.

Disadvantages of following an RFP Process

- The process can use up a lot of resource time.
- The vendor selection process can be tedious.
- Requires engagement and sign off from departments
  like; Finance, Legal, and Procurement.

Why some organizations don't use RFPs

Depending on the size of your organization, it may not make
sense to have an RFP process in place. For example, if you
are purchasing 20 new laptops, it may not make sense to run
a whole RFP process due to the low cost of the purchase. The
time and efforts put into an RFP process can outweigh the
asset procurement costs themselves.

A scenario where running an RFP process would make sense
would be when an organization is spending a significant
amount of money on new assets. For example, an
organization may be upgrading their data center storage
infrastructure, which could include 200 new cutting-edge

servers. If the market price for those servers are $6000 each, then it makes sense to get the best price as you could be spending a total of $1,200,000 on the purchase.

Most organizations setup a minimum financial threshold before an RFP can be generated. This eliminates low dollar purchases from going through the time intensive process of an RFP.

Sending out an RFP

The final stage of completing an RFP is sending it to your vendors. The best method of delivery is usually via email. After the RFP has been submitted, you should receive an acknowledgment, followed by responses, as per your defined deadline date.

Request for Quote (RFQ)

The final stage of procuring assets is to issue a Request for Quote (RFQ) to all preferred vendors.

The purpose of the RFQ is to obtain multiples quotes for the purchase, and to select a vendor that fits your requirements, and budget.

Once the quotes are received, all involved parties must then select a vendor for the purchase. After a selection has been made, the Chief Financial Officer (CFO) usually has to approve or reject the purchase request. Once the CFO approves the purchase request, the procurement department then issues a Purchase Order (PO) to the selected vendor to proceed with the purchase.

Depending on your organization and procurement policies, these steps may vary from the process described above. The reason for this is every organization is different, and not all businesses operate in the same manner, especially when it comes to the procurement of goods or services. This is especially true if you are a government organization, as stricter rules and regulations are normally put in place.

Once the vendor has received the purchase order, and received payment, the vendor will then ship the asset(s) to the location specified by the purchaser. When the assets are delivered to the premises, depending on the urgency, they are generally delivered directly to the Asset Management storeroom. This ensures that assets are; physically verified against the purchase order, tagged, securely stored, and logged in the asset inventory.

Purchase Order (PO) Explained

A **Purchase Order (PO)** is a document issued to a vendor from a buyer, which lists out all of the assets that the buyer wishes to purchase. A Purchase Order (PO) usually lists out the following information for each individual item; price, item quantity, serial number, model, product SKU, and a detailed description.

Vendor Management

In IT Asset Management, managing the vendors that you procure assets from is a vital component when running an IT Asset Management program. Maintaining accurate records of all vendors can help mitigate possible future issues, and is also a great way to track the point of contact for each vendor that the organization is involved with.

Vendor Scorecard

The **Vendor Scorecard** is a document that is used by internal teams of the organization to log and track the performance of all vendors. The ultimate goal of a Vendor Scorecard is to educate stakeholders of an organization with the overall grade/score of a vendor.

A Vendor Scorecard typically evaluates a vendor's performance based on the following areas:

- Pricing
- Payment terms
- Quality of products
- Shipping time
- Purchase Order (PO) errors
- Email response time
- Quality of communication

Each time a Purchase Order (PO) is made and received from a vendor, the IT and/or Procurement department will update the vendor scorecard with grades for each area. Typically, vendor scorecards use a grading system (A-F), which translate to percentages. The higher the overall percentage of a vendor, the better they rank.

Vendor Scorecards are excellent to use in IT Asset Management, as they give the Procurement department a clear idea of which vendor is best suited for each Purchase Order (PO). This enables organizations to make clear, and informed decisions when it comes to the procurement of new assets or services.

Asset Receiving

Asset Receiving is the process when IT Asset Managers receive newly purchased assets. Assets are usually received when a shipping courier, or vendor delivers new assets to the organization. The Asset Manager is responsible for verifying that all assets on the Purchase Order (PO) are present at the time of delivery. Depending on the organization that you work for, this document may come in the form of a Bill of Materials (BOM), or Bill of Quantity (BOQ). If a delivery contains documentation mistakes, or missing items, then they should be documented and communicated to the finance department.

Running a visual inspection of all assets at the point of receiving is also recommended as an Asset Management best practice. This ensures that any damaged goods are identified before signing off on the delivery. If damaged goods are found, then the courier or vendor can return the assets there and then. Signing off on a delivery of assets indicates that you are happy and accept the delivered goods. If problems occur after signing off on a delivery, then it becomes more difficult to resolve the issue as the vendor may contest that the assets were not damaged at the point of delivery.

Asset Tagging

What is an Asset Tag?

An **Asset Tag** is an alphanumeric barcoded label that is applied to hardware assets for the purpose of tracking and identification. Asset tags typically include 1D or 2D barcodes, and usually contain the name or logo of the business. Asset tags assist with the scanning and reconciliation of hardware assets, and help speed up entry of data.

Implementing Asset Tags

Imagine trying to inventory a room full of hundreds if not thousands of assets. Without asset tags, the process would be manual and painstaking. You would have to manually read each serial number off each device and then type it into your repository system to pull up the record. With asset tags, you can enter a room, and easily start scanning assets with a barcode scanner.

Asset tags are extremely useful for businesses because they make the logging of asset movements and changes easier. For example in a Data Center, servers are frequently transferred. Asset tags allow IT Engineers to easily scan the device into the repository, and change the location and/or status in real-time.

Benefits of using asset tags

The following are just a few benefits of using asset tags in an Asset Management program:

- Deters people from stealing assets
- Aligns the organization with industry standards and audit requirements
- Assigns a unique ID to each asset
- Prevents data entry errors
- Quicker asset tracking and inventorying
- Allows people to easily identify if it's a company owned asset

What type of asset tag is best for your organization?

Depending on the industry type of your organization, different types of asset tags are best suited more than others. For example if your assets are situated in hot conditions, consider purchasing aluminum asset tags as these are heat resistant and rigid. Whereas if your assets are located in cool conditions and don't move around much, then regular foil or polyester asset tags will work just fine.

RFID Tags

Radio-frequency Identification (RFID) asset tags are a more convenient, but expensive alternative to traditional asset tags. RFID asset tags contain a chip that allow information to be passed through radio waves. RFID tags consist of two different types; active, and passive.

In Asset Management, RFID tags can be used to easily inventory a room to validate its contents in a matter of seconds. Implementing an RFID asset management system requires additional equipment such as; antennas and readers.

A **Passive RFID Tag** is a tag that only transmits a signal when an RFID reader is present. The benefit of using a passive RFID tag is that it doesn't contain a battery, and uses energy from an RFID reader when in contact. Passive RFID tags are popular due to their low cost when compared to active RFID tags.

An **Active RFID Tag** is a tag that is always transmitting a signal, and requires a battery for it to operate. Active RFID tags usually run on 433 MHz and 915 MHz wave lengths. One of the reasons why active RFID tags are popular is because of their long read range capability, but at the same time, they are generally a lot more expensive than passive RFID tags. This means organizations can detect and track their assets from a far distance, when using Active RFID tags.

When making a decision on what type of RFID tags to use, you should weigh out the advantages and disadvantages, as active RFID tags require more maintenance and support, whereas passive RFID tags don't require maintenance.

Deciding on the location of RFID readers is an important decision to make when implementing an RFID tracking system. Installing readers in areas with high foot traffic will ensure updates happen more frequently, and will enable the Asset Repository to have up-to-date location data.

It is recommended that the following areas have RFID readers installed:

- Major entrances
- Major exits
- Entry and exits of all asset storerooms
- Data center doorways

GPS Tracking

Global Positioning System (GPS) technology is an additional type of technology that can be used to track hardware assets.

GPS tracking is best for assets that are constantly moving around, and are never static in the same place. GPS tracking in IT Asset Management is an additional tracking method that is usually used for tracking only certain types of assets. The benefit of using GPS technology is that it can update the asset repository in near real-time, providing exact location information.

GPS tracking is an expensive alternative to using RFID technology, but can provide much more visibility. GPS tracking is also important because it can; deter theft, help recover lost or stolen assets, improve accountability, and track movement and usage.

Placement of Asset Tags

The location of an asset tag on a device is crucial, the tag should be located in such a place that is easily accessible and clearly visible while the asset is in operation. Before applying asset tags to all of the inventory, first decide where to apply the asset tag on each device. Remember, after the asset tag is applied, it can be difficult to remove.

Take a server for example, if the asset tag was applied on the top or bottom of the chassis, then it would be inaccessible when it's installed in a rack. Whereas if you apply the asset tag on the front plate of a server, it will be easily accessible for locating and scanning while in operation. These types of decisions can make a big impact on the operations of an Asset Management program.

When you are ready to start applying asset tags, the surface must be free of dust or dirt, as this can affect the durability of the tag, and it may easily fall off in the future if applied to a dirty surface.

Note: Before starting this process, ensure everyone on the Asset Management team involved are aware and properly trained to tag assets. Be careful not to cover important information and/or air intake holes when applying asset tags, as this can damage the asset in the long run.

Asset Redeployment

Asset Redeployment is the activity when existing assets are returned, and then later re-deployed for operation. Asset Redeployment helps organizations save vast amounts of money, and also assists with helping the environment.

There are many forms of asset redeployment. For example, an employee may return their laptop to the IT Help Desk for the purpose of upgrading. At the same time, a manager may request a laptop for a new employee. That new employee may not require the latest and greatest hardware, so in this scenario, the returned laptop can be redeployed, and cost savings are instantly gained.

Other benefits of asset redeployment include the following:

- Increased lifetime of an asset
- Increased Return on Investment (ROI)
- Decreased carbon footprint
- Reduced asset spend
- Reduced environmental waste
- Reduced asset storage costs

Tracking redeployed assets is an important practice in IT Asset Management as it showcases to the CFO and other stakeholders that real cost savings are occurring. With financial data present in the Asset Repository, the IT Asset Management department can easily run reports to show the exact dollar amount saved for any given financial year. When this type of data is presented to the Finance department, trust is gained from the CFO, and the use-case for IT Asset Management is further strengthened and supported.

The asset redeployment process can be tricky, which is why determining whether or not to redeploy an asset is an important part of the decision making process. For some assets, it's more practical to redeploy them back into operation because of their financial value, but for other assets, the associated maintenance and support costs can greatly outweigh the expected cost savings. The cost of shipping is also another factor to consider when redeploying assets as it may cost more than the asset itself, in such an occasion, consider local procurement as an alternative for the requestor.

Asset Storeroom

Storerooms are designated areas where assets are held for the purpose of storage. Storerooms allow the Asset Management team to securely store assets when they are not in use. The benefits of a storeroom are that they allow Asset Managers to easily store large amounts of devices, in a contained space. Storerooms typically have lots of shelves and drawers. Good storage equipment allow Asset Managers to easily and conveniently store and locate assets when requests arise.

The asset storeroom is an excellent way to ensure that assets are securely in the custody of the IT Asset Management team. Storing spare assets in closets, desks, and cupboards is bad practice. When IT Engineers store assets in off-the-record storage locations, the IT Asset Management team doesn't have visibility that they are there, and not in-use. This can cost the organization money because other IT teams may purchase the same assets, therefore generating unnecessary spend.

Stock distribution is an important success factor in ensuring the asset management team can fulfil asset requests successfully, and more importantly, on time. For example, let's say an organization has three large buildings, one is for IT operations, and the other two are for employee training. If each building has an asset storeroom, it would be best to place the majority of IT operation-related assets in the designated IT Operations storeroom. This will ensure that asset requests are fulfilled quicker, engineers can respond faster, and the downtime of IT systems is reduced.

By introducing an asset storeroom, organizations can benefit from the following:

- A single collection point for asset requests
- Temperature controlled environment
- Safe and secure storage
- Reduced IT system downtime
- Easily monitor all available assets
- Meet regularity and security compliance standards

Authorized Personnel

Another key component to securely managing a storeroom is to designate access to authorized personnel only. This will prevent unauthorized access and asset check-outs. By limiting the number of employees with access to the stockroom, the risk of losing track of equipment in-stock is reduced, and increases accountability within the Asset Management program.

Deploying Assets

When IT Engineers collect assets from a storeroom, an asset checkout record should be logged in the asset repository and signed by the IT Engineer who collected the assets. The checkout form should include the following information:

- Deployed By (Name)
- Deployed To (Name)
- Deployment Location
- Serial Number(s)
- Part Number(s)
- Asset Tags(s)
- End User Name (If applicable)
- End User Cost Center

- Approved By (Name)
- Signatures from all parties

Before an asset is checked out and deployed, the IT Asset Management team must ensure that the asset request has been approved by the appropriate person. Typically when IT equipment is being requested and deployed, it is the manager of the requesting employee that is required to give approval. If the equipment is not intended for end users and is for a project, then the IT Manager, or Project Manager must approve the asset request. Going through an approval process ensures that assets are not incorrectly deployed, and every request is accounted for. Many times in storerooms, assets that are owned by other departments are accidently issued to users from other departments. By introducing a formal request and approval process, assets can be issued appropriately.

IT Service Catalog

The **IT Service Catalog** is a digital catalog that contains all IT services that an organization provides to its employees. The catalog is used by all employees of an organization to request IT services, and/or devices. Once a request is made through an IT Service Catalog, it is usually then sent directly to the IT Help Desk for fulfillment.

In IT Asset Management, the service catalog is used specifically for employees to select assets that they need. Typically, the catalog is connected to the Asset Repository, this enables the catalog to know what assets are in-stock, and available at the requesters location.

In most organizations, the IT Service Catalog is available to all employees via an internal web portal. The web portal then allows users to easily navigate and select services and/or assets that they need. The Service Catalog also provides

Service Level Agreement (SLA) information for each IT service and asset request, this ensures that the requestor knows when the service or asset request will be fulfilled.

In some organizations, it is common that when a request is placed, it is then sent to the requestor's manager for approval. This ensures that all requests are approved and accounted for. Typically, the service catalog is configured in a way where only items over a certain cost require approval. For example, it wouldn't make sense to obtain an approval for a $20 headset, whereas it would for an $1800 laptop. The approval process ensures all requests are accounted for, and no surprise chargebacks are later discovered.

Although the IT Help Desk and IT Service Management (ITSM) departments are usually responsible for the management of the IT Service Catalog, the IT Asset Management team is involved due to the asset fulfillment side behind the catalog.

Depending on the size and complexity of an organization, some IT Service Catalogs display different services and assets depending on the rank of the employee. For example, a C-Level Executive may get special access to exclusive assets and services, whereas a Salesman may only have access to regular assets and services. This can vary depending on the size of an organization, and the agreed upon Service Level Agreements (SLAs).

Introducing an IT Service Catalog can benefit an organization in the following ways:

- Simplifies the interaction between IT Help Desk and the IT Asset Management team
- Creates transparency around available assets and fulfillment timeframes
- Provides insight into the cost of an asset
- Creates a positive user experience for end users
- Gives end users visibility into their requests

Managing Consumables

Consumables, also known as accessories, are assets that are not required to be tracked while in-use due to their low value and ease of replacement. Consumables consist of assets such as:

- Cables and adapters
- Earphones
- Printer cartridges and toners
- Laptop locks
- Keyboards
- Mice
- Webcams

Since consumables are not tracked after deployment, it is unusual for consumables to be asset tagged. Most organizations decide not to track consumables due to their low value. Consumables should be tracked when they are purchased and kept in storage, this ensures that all IT Asset Managers have visibility over all of the in-stock consumables.

Generally speaking, when tracking consumables in the asset repository, the following attributes should be captured:

- Manufacturer
- Part number/SKU
- Description
- Quantity
- Vendor
- Storeroom

Although most consumables have serial numbers, logging such level of detail is not necessary.

When deploying a consumable via an Asset Fulfillment Request, it is best practice to include the part number, description, assigned user, and quantity on the Asset Check-

Out form. Tracking this level of information ensures that each consumable deployed is accounted for.

It is also common for some organizations to make consumables available via vending machines. Introducing vending machines allows end users to easily obtain new accessories when old ones fail, and reduces the support needed from the IT Help Desk. Since consumables don't require the same amount of governance and tracking as hardware assets do, organizations are able to deploy accessories in a more self-service like approach.

Standards and Frameworks

Over the years, Standards and Frameworks have been designed and published around IT Asset Management (ITAM) best practices. To this date, several international bodies provide standards around IT Asset Management, and its related subjects.

The benefit of using Standards and Frameworks in an organization is to align processes and controls around industry standards. This ensures that all activities and functions are performed correctly.

Information Technology Infrastructure Library (ITIL)

Information Technology Infrastructure Library (ITIL) is a set of processes designed around IT Service Management (ITSM). The goal of ITIL is to align IT Services with the needs of an organization.

ITIL was introduced by the UK government in the 1980s because of a lack of quality IT Services available. The standard was designed and introduced to ensure better quality services were made available.

The ITIL methodology consists of five stages that create the ITIL Service Lifecycle:

- Service Strategy
- Service Design
- Service Transition
- Service Operation
- Continual Service Improvement

IT Asset Management is considered to be a small sub-section of the ITIL Framework, which derives from the Service Asset and Configuration Management (SACM) process. SACM covers the best practices of configuration management, and instructs organizations on how to maintain an accurate Configuration Management Database (CMDB).

Since IT Asset Management and Configuration Management are closely related, learning and implementing the ITIL Framework can greatly benefit an organization.

ISO 27001

ISO 27001 is an international information security standard created to support organizations with their Information Security Management System (ISMS). ISO 27001 specifically focuses on the legal, technical, and physical controls of an organization. The standard covers the management and security of IT Assets within an organization.

IT Asset Management is tightly coupled with ISO 27001, as the accuracy of tracking assets directly influences the success of achieving ISO 27001 compliancy.

ISO 19770

ISO 19770 is the family of international standards relating to the management of software and related IT assets. The standard primarily focuses on Software Asset Management (SAM), but also covers subjects around the management of hardware assets. The standard also places heavy focus on the importance of providing a quality asset management program, in order to ensure smooth operations for IT Service Management (ITSM).

Configuration Management Database (CMDB)

The **Configuration Management Database (CMDB)** is a database that stores all of an organization's IT asset installations, also known as Configuration Items (CI). A **Configuration Item (CI)** is a configuration record that relates to an IT asset and stores its attributes and purpose. The CMDB contains all of an organizations critical assets to ensure asset and service dependencies are accurately mapped, and accounted for.

Dependencies in a CMDB are mapped as downstream or upstream relationships between one and another. Dependencies are defined by how a particular system or configuration of assets are connected together, and what business service they support.

An example of a simple Configuration Item (CI) relationship in a CMDB could be an Email Service. The Email Service depends on the operation of a server to support the service. The server supporting the service would be classed as a downstream dependency, if the server encounters an incident or a problem, then the email service may be affected. This type of information greatly supports IT Engineers with impact analysis, and resolving service and infrastructure issues.

Configuration Items (CI) include the following:

- IT Assets
- Software
- Contract Agreements
- Business Services
- People
- Documentation
- Locations

Configuration Items have the following attributes:

- Configuration Name
- Configuration Number
- Description
- Owner
- Importance
- Support Group
- Relationship
- Item Type
- Vendor
- Operating System
- IP Address

Depending on the type of configuration item you are tracking, different attributes will be available for capturing. For example, the configuration item of a server will allow an IT engineer to track the operating system, whereas a contract agreement will allow a contract admin to track the vendor.

Most asset repositories have a Configuration Management Database (CMDB) system built in, this allows users to automatically create configuration items when assets are being created.

Depending on the size of an organization, and the dependency of systems, some organizations may not require or need a CMDB. However, some organizations may only track critical configuration items, as tracking and maintaining a CMDB for every IT asset can be an overkill.

The Configuration Management Database (CMDB) is also a key element of the IT Infrastructure Library (ITIL). ITIL explains the CMDB as being a main component for the success of supporting an organization's IT infrastructure. The CMDB is important when it relates to Incident, Problem and Change Management, as IT Engineers can easily identify what related assets and services are affected when an issue or change is logged.

Benefits of a Configuration Management Database (CMDB)

Implementing and maintaining an up-to-date CMDB can benefit an organization by the following:

- Faster root cause analysis
- Faster incident resolution
- Single reference point for all IT Asset and Service dependencies
- Helps correlate events to infrastructure issues
- Helps identify risks before implementing changes
- Identifies duplicate systems and can drive down IT spend

Warranties

A **Warranty** is a contract agreement between a manufacturer, and an organization that promises the repair or replacement of an asset when it becomes damaged. Warranties are typically issued free of charge for a set period of time when an asset is purchased new from a manufacturer.

Warranties usually cover:

- Problems not caused by the owner
- Defective software
- Damaged hardware due to normal wear and tear

Warranties usually don't cover:

- Replacement of lost or stolen assets
- Data recovery
- Damage directly caused by the owner

In IT Asset Management, warranties are extremely crucial as they cover the support needed to fix assets when they face unexpected issues. The management and tracking of all warranties is a key factor in successfully implementing and managing an IT Asset Management program. With the use of warranties, the IT Help Desk can outsource most hardware issues back to the manufacturer. This reduces the overall IT spend, and allows organizations to re-allocate resources to other issues.

Benefits of warranties:

- Reduced IT maintenance support costs
- Peace of mind for an organization
- No unexpected repair costs
- Reduced asset downtime
- Reduced Total Cost of Ownership (TCO)

In IT Asset Management, it's important that warranties are logged in the asset repository when assets are procured and received. This ensures that the IT Department are aware of any warranty support available.

Depending on the manufacturer, some issue warranties digitally, and others issue physical warranty cards. If you receive a warranty card for an asset, ensure it is scanned and stored in the asset repository, this will verify the warranties validity, even if the warranty card is lost or stolen.

Warranty cards usually include the following attributes:

- Warranty Start Date
- Warranty Duration
- Serial Number
- Part Number
- Manufacturer Name

Sometimes, warranties can be voided if unauthorized repair work is carried out on an asset. Depending on the type of device, some assets include a warranty label that is applied to the edge of an asset's chassis, if the asset has been dismantled, and the label is damaged, then any associated warranties are usually voided.

The warranty void label is used to indicate to a manufacturer that a device has been opened and possibly tampered with. This safeguards manufacturers from issuing support to organizations who may have caused damage themselves.

The terms and conditions of warranties are also very important to pay attention to. Depending on the type of warranty supplied, some manufacturers place strict terms that specify when and how an asset can be repaired whilst under warranty. For example, it is very common that laptop and computer warranties are only valid within the country of purchase, meaning if a laptop was purchased in India, but later transferred to the United States, the laptop most likely won't be supported in the United States.

Extended Warranties

An **Extended Warranty** is a warranty that a manufacturer sells after the standard factory warranty has expired. Extended warranties offer organizations additional peace of mind for their IT assets, and cover them when support is required. Since extended warranties are typically purchased somewhere after 3-5 years from the original purchase date, the warranties themselves can be quite expensive, therefore not all organizations opt for extended warranties.

Depending on the amount of locations that an organization has and the distribution of core assets, the cost of extended warranties can be worth it. For example, if a large grocery store has over 300 locations, and there is no IT support in each location, it would be wise to purchase extended warranties for critical assets, as the cost to send internal IT Engineers to distant or remote locations can become costly.

KPIs and Metrics

Tracking and monitoring the metrics of an IT Asset Management program are crucial for the overall success of an

ITAM initiative. Metrics are key for measuring and identifying the successes of a program.

A metric is a specific measure that gauges the performance of a particular activity or task. Some examples of quantifiable metrics are;

- Assets purchased over the last 30 days or
- Assets deployed this week

Without metrics, members of the organization would struggle to determine factors such as:

- The efficiency of the ITAM program
- Total cost savings achieved
- How can the ITAM program be improved

By creating meaningful metrics and Key Performance Indicators (KPIs), all ITAM stakeholders can easily monitor the overall health of the ITAM program. Defined metrics benefit the organization through gaining support, justifying business decisions, showcasing cost savings, monitoring productivity, displaying the Return on Investment (ROI), and identifying problems.

When defining metrics for an ITAM program, ensure they are meaningful to the target audience. Metrics and KPIs should aim to drive specific business outcomes. For example, the Chief Financial Officer (CFO), may not be interested in the quantity of assets in maintenance, whereas the IT Manager would have interest. This type of information could be useful to an IT Manager because it may alert him or her about an unknown issue.

Typically in most Asset Repositories, the ability to customize and display KPIs is a common feature. When setting up an Asset Repository, ensure to display meaningful KPIs as it will encourage and drive the ITAM team to success.

Below are examples of IT Asset Management KPIs that are commonly used across organizations.

KPI	Metric Type
Average lifetime of an asset	Duration
Average time to fulfill an asset request	Duration
Average time assets are held in-stock	Duration
Total cost of assets purchased this month	Financial
Average cost of asset requests	Financial
Total savings achieved this year through asset re-use	Financial
IT Asset Chargeback applied this month	Financial
Percentage of assets in-use	Quantity
Assets added to the repository this month	Quantity
Assets deployed this month	Quantity

Metrics and KPIs are the drivers behind:

- Increased productivity
- Meaningful discussions
- Identifying inefficiencies
- Accountability

Overall, metrics and KPIs are a fantastic way to share and celebrate team success, and to showcase to other departments the accomplishments achieved.

Lastly, without KPIs and Metrics, there wouldn't be any way to gauge and benchmark the success of an ITAM program. Implementing KPIs and Metrics are paramount when developing an effective ITAM implementation.

Reporting

The use of reporting in IT Asset Management is a crucial driver for the success of an ITAM program. Reports can easily identify issues and inform members of the organization accordingly. Reports are also great to share with other departments when showcasing the efforts of the ITAM team, or when presenting issues.

Reports are also great ways to keep teams on track. For example, if a report is sent to the IT Help Desk displaying all assets that were deployed the previous week without chargeback, this will drive the IT Help Desk to identify and resolve any issues. This style of reporting prompts teams to fix issues before they become major problems.

Reports are useful for uncovering issues such as:

- Data input errors
- Process inefficiencies
- Unnecessary expenses
- Security vulnerabilities
- Service Level Agreement (SLA) breaches

Excessive Reporting

It is possible to have too many reports, when designing reports for the IT Asset Management team, try to limit the number of reports. Having too many reports can make the ITAM operations more complicated then they need to be.

Ensure all reports that you create actually hold value and drive business outcomes. Too many times organizations create pretty looking reports, but fail to gain any benefit from them. Before designing and creating any reports, sit down and write down the business outcomes and objectives that you wish to gain from the reports. With a list of all business outcomes and objectives documented, this will then help you come up with meaningful reports that drive actions.

Examples of useful IT Asset Management reports:

Report	Audience	Action It Drives
Critical assets that are low in-stock	IT Help Desk	Informs IT Department to procure more assets
Assets in-stock	IT Help Desk	Informs IT Department of available assets that can be used for deployment
In-use machines without an assigned user	IT Help Desk IT Asset Management Team	Ensures the ITAM team assign assets to their users
In-use machines without any associated chargebacks	IT Help Desk Finance	Informs IT Department of possible process errors or loopholes Helps identify and recover overlooked IT chargebacks
Deployed machines that haven't been used for over 2 months	IT Help Desk	Informs IT Department of assets that can be redeployed

Deployed assets without asset tags	IT Asset Management Team	Informs the ITAM team of a possible process error
Assets with expiring warranties (next 3 months)	IT Help Desk	Drives the IT Help Desk to purchase extended warranties
Assets with expired warranties	IT Help Desk	Informs the IT Help Desk of assets that are no longer covered by the manufacturer
Assets scheduled for maintenance	IT Help Desk	Informs the IT Help Desk to run maintenance
Damaged assets by location	IT Help Desk IT Asset Management Team	Informs the IT Help Desk of any possible problematic locations that are causing damage to assets
Leased assets in-use after the lease return date	IT Help Desk IT Asset Management Team	Alerts IT Department of any breached lease agreements, and informs them to return assets back to the manufacturer/vendor
Assets with out of date and/or blacklisted software	IT Help Desk IT Security	Alerts IT and Security of machines that pose security risks
Users with more than one	IT Help Desk	Informs IT Department of users with too many assets

laptop or computer		Enables IT Department to collect and redeploy assets
Asset records with a duplicate serial number or asset tag	IT Asset Management Team	Informs the ITAM team of possible data errors
Asset fulfillment requests that have been open for more than two weeks	IT Asset Management Team	Informs the ITAM team of any forgotten or unknown asset requests
Asset fulfillment requests that breached the defined ITAM SLA	IT Asset Management Team	Informs the ITAM team of possible fulfillment process issues

Typically, most Asset Repositories come with reporting functionalities out of the box. These types of reports are very useful because they don't require any setup or complex development effort.

Depending on the type of data displayed in a report, reports can be displayed in all different shapes and sizes. Among some the most common types of reports are; spreadsheets, line graphs, pie charts, and bar charts.

Automated Reporting

Automated Reporting is a great way for IT Asset Managers, and members of the IT Asset Management team to receive and be informed of issues or tasks that require action. Automated reports are typically triggered via the asset repository in the form of an email notification.

Automated reports are most effective for members of the ITAM team to be alerted on the following issues and request types:

- Storerooms with insufficient assets in stock
- Asset fulfillment requests
- Recently placed purchase orders
- Assets that have changed ownership
- Deployed assets without associated chargeback

Processing Returned Assets

In most organizations, IT Assets are returned to the IT Asset Management department for the purpose of storage when they are no longer in-use. Assets are typically returned to the IT Asset Management team when one of the following events has occurred:

- An employee leaves the company
- A technology refresh has taken place, and new hardware has been installed
- Assets have been identified as no longer in-use

Once assets have been identified for return, the IT Engineering team and/or IT Help Desk return the assets to the storeroom specified by the IT Asset Management team. When receiving assets, it is best practice to always fill out an Asset Return form. The Asset Return form is used to officially document the return of assets, and to capture the following information:

- Assets Received By (Name and Signature)

- Assets Returned By (Name and Signature)
- Date and Time
- Asset Tag
- Serial Number
- Part Number
- Condition
- Storeroom Received In

Once the Asset Return form has been completed and signed, the custody of the assets are then officially transferred to the IT Asset Management department. By implementing an Asset Return form, the IT Asset Management team has an official record of the assets returned, and condition of them.

After an asset return has taken place, it is essential to upload a copy of the Asset Return form to the Asset Repository, this ensures that the transaction record is available for future inquiries or audits.

Depending on the specific policies of an organization, it is common practice for some companies to actually charge the employee for not returning assets upon leaving the company. This policy is designed to safeguard organizations from financial loss caused by the non-return of company owned assets.

Managing Leased Assets

In most organizations, it is common for the IT department to lease certain types of assets from a manufacturer. By leasing assets from a manufacturer, the Total Cost of Ownership (TCO) can be reduced as the manufacturer is responsible for the maintenance and support of the devices. In most cases, IT departments will lease devices such as computers and laptops.

In some scenarios, it is much cheaper for organizations to lease IT equipment, as opposed to purchasing them. Many manufacturers now offer attractive leasing packages, accompanied with low monthly rates.

Benefits of leasing assets:

- Reduces Total Cost of Ownership (TCO)
- Allows organizations to switch IT spend from Capital Expenditure (CAPEX) to Operational Expenditure (OPEX)
- Simplifies IT Chargeback
- Drives IT Asset Management initiatives
- Enables organizations to easily downsize the amount of devices at any time
- Supplies organizations with the latest and greatest technology

The industry term for leasing computers and laptops is generally referred to as **PC as a Service (PCaaS)**. PCaaS is similar to Software as a Service (SaaS), because the manufacturer or vendor supplies the equipment and service, in exchange for a monthly fee. This type of model is highly attractive as it allows IT departments to free up Capital Expenditure (CAPEX), and move to Operational Expenditure (OPEX).

When negotiating a leasing agreement with a manufacturer, be sure to check the terms and conditions of the contract, as some lease agreements can contain penalties if assets are lost, stolen, or returned damaged.

At the end of a lease agreement, manufacturers usually offer four options:

- Purchase the leased assets
- Keep the assets, and extend the lease agreement at a reduced rate
- Return the leased assets
- Refresh the leased assets with new ones and renew the lease agreement

When returning leased assets back to a manufacturer, it is crucial to make sure that all of the assets are still present in the organization, and not lost. It is best practice to run a true-up process of the inventory using a discovery tool to identify possible missing assets. This prepares the organization for any financial implications that the manufacturer may impose.

Once all assets have been identified, the IT Help Desk should wipe all data off the devices, as this ensures that no sensitive data can leave the organization. In this process, software applications should also be removed, and re-used elsewhere.

Processing Lost or Stolen Assets

In the world of IT, assets are always moving around and are constantly exposed to risk throughout their lifetime. End user deployed assets are the most common types of assets that are exposed to being lost or stolen. End user assets can consist of devices such as;

- Laptops
- Cell Phones
- Tablets
- External Hard Drives

Due to the portability of end user devices, it is common for unattended assets to get lost, or even stolen while outside an organization. The tracking and management of lost or stolen assets is a process in itself within IT Asset Management, and requires thorough attention to detail.

Typically within an organization, employees should immediately report lost or stolen assets to the IT Help Desk. The reporting of lost or stolen assets should be part of all employee policies, this ensures that all employees are aware of the process, and understand what to do when an asset is lost or stolen.

When the IT Help Desk are notified of an incident, they should immediately inform the IT Asset Management department and the **Security Operations Center (SOC)**. This ensures that all appropriate departments are notified, and can take the required action.

Informing the SOC department is a very important part of the asset lost or stolen process, as they determine the security risk of an incident, and take all appropriate actions to protect the information of an organization (in the case of a data leak).

In IT Asset Management, when an asset is reported to be lost or stolen, the first step is to file an official police report in the country where the incident took place. This is typically done by the custodian of the asset (end user), and should be done immediately after an incident has occurred. Once the police report has been filed, this then acts as an official document authenticating the event.

The second step is for the IT Asset Manager to complete the asset lost or stolen form. The asset lost or stolen form is an official document within an organization that contains all of the relevant information of the incident. This document can be used when filing claims with insurance companies, and as an official record documenting the incident.

The asset lost or stolen form typically includes the following information:

- Employee Name
- Incident Location (Address, City, and Country)
- Date
- Asset Type (Laptop, Cell phone etc.)
- Asset Tag
- Serial Number
- Estimated Value
- Police Report Number

After completing the asset lost or stolen form, the IT Asset Management department should inform the Finance department of the incident, and provide a copy of the completed lost or stolen form. This allows the Finance department to officially write-off the asset in their accounting system, and to log it as stolen. This ensures that the Finance department no longer apply depreciation to the particular asset, and logs the asset as a total loss.

The final stage of processing a lost or stolen asset is to update the asset repository. All assets that have been lost or stolen should be updated to reflect their new status as either lost or stolen. It is also best practice to attach a copy of the completed asset lost or stolen form and to include the police report. This ensures that the IT Asset Management department has all of the evidence for all lost and/or stolen assets, and can be used for audit inquiries in the future.

In some cases lost or stolen assets can be used by criminals to engage in illegal, or fraudulent activities. Therefore logging and documenting all lost and stolen assets can protect organizations both legally and financially.

Asset Disposal and Recycling

Disposing of IT assets can seem like a daunting task, especially if you are planning on removing thousands of IT assets from your organization. During the asset disposal process, concerns over security, transportation, and disposal costs are not unusual. By following a systemic process known as **IT Asset Disposition (ITAD)**, it can be a simple and stress-free process.

Communicating with Stakeholders

Before any assets can be disposed, it's important to work with the stakeholders from each related department to understand and identify which assets need to be disposed. Assets are most commonly identified for disposal when they no longer hold any functional value to the organization, as keeping assets that are not needed costs money.

The process for identifying assets for disposal often takes place within the Asset Repository. Within the Asset Repository, IT Managers identify and mark off assets that are no longer needed. When selecting assets for disposal, IT Managers typically look for assets that match any one of the following characteristics:

- The asset no longer meets organizational needs
- The asset no longer provides any functional value
- The asset is broken and unrepairable or
- The asset is broken but the cost of repair is too high

Flagging assets for disposal in the Asset Repository can be simple. In most asset repositories, an asset status field can be used to identify that the asset is ready for disposal.

Once all stakeholders have completed identifying all assets for disposal, the next stage is to receive sign-off from the Chief Technology Officer (CTO), and the Chief Financial Officer (CFO). Receiving sign-off from these members of the organization will ensure the disposal has been approved from the highest level of authority. Depending on the policies put in place by an organization, this level of sign-off may not be required; this comes down to the size of the company, and the financial policies put in place.

Removing Data

The next step in the disposal process is to wipe data from all assets that have the ability to store data. The following types of assets have the ability to store data:

- Computers
- Laptops
- Servers
- Mobile Phones

- Tablets
- Hard Drives

The above devices are just a few examples of the types of assets that have the ability to store data. Using the Asset Repository, it is recommended that you flag asset categories that have the ability to store data; this will make the disposal process of assets much easier.

Before any assets are wiped of their data, ensure that the IT team removes any software installed on the devices. This will drive software re-use, and will save the organization money on software licensing. Failure to remove software licenses from disposed assets could lead to complicated true-up processes, and affect any future software vendor audits.

When all assets with the ability to store data have been identified, it is recommended that you work with the IT Help Desk team to have all data wiped from these devices. This will ensure that confidential data does not leave the organization's premises. This then secures the organization from any possible data breaches that could occur.

If the assets are going to be destructed by an IT Asset Disposition (ITAD) vendor, and not sold for re-use, then its best practice to have any hard drives or storage tapes degaussed. A **Degausser** is a machine that exposes a powerful magnetic field to the asset that is placed on it. The magnetic field that is exposed to the hard drive or tape then removes any magnetic field from the device. This then removes any data that is stored on the device. Degaussing is an irreversible process, once an asset has been degaussed, it's then unusable for future use.

Before deciding to use an IT Asset Disposition (ITAD) vendor, consider re-selling the assets or donating them to a charity. Selling or donating assets all depends on the condition of them. If in working order, donating or selling the assets may be the best route to take. Donating assets is a good technique to increase the positive reputation of an organization. Selling assets (also known as repurposing) is a great way to dispose of assets, this enables companies to retrieve funds to help support the purchase of new assets. This decision ultimately comes down to the organization's policies and procedures put in place.

Working with an IT Asset Disposition (ITAD) Vendor

The next step in the Asset Disposition process is to work with a reliable IT Asset Disposition vendor. An ITAD vendor is typically responsible for the following:

- Collecting assets
- Packaging assets
- Transporting assets securely to their disposal facility
- Selling assets (when applicable)
- Destructing assets
- Generating an Asset Destruction Certificate
- Generating a Data Destruction Report
- Recycling asset materials

If your organization doesn't already have a contract with an ITAD vendor, there are a wide variety available in the marketplace that offer low cost IT Asset Disposition (ITAD) services. Some ITAD vendors even offer onsite asset destruction, this gives the organization peace of mind that all assets are securely destructed even before leaving the premises.

Once you have established a relationship or contract with an ITAD vendor, arrange a convenient time with them for the collection of your assets. Ensure that the Asset Repository is updated throughout the disposition process, this will ensure that all assets reflect their actual status and whereabouts. Before assets are collected by an ITAD vendor, ensure that all asset tags are removed from the assets. This will ensure that if any assets get lost or stolen on the way to the disposal facility, this will safeguard the organization from being associated with those assets.

After the ITAD vendor has collected the assets from an organization, the vendor will then deliver the assets to their secure facility. Within the facility, the assets will then be stripped down of their components and set aside for recycling. Parts capable of storing data are usually shredded to prevent future re-use.

Following the destruction of the assets, the ITAD vendor will then generate an Asset Destruction Certificate. The certificate typically includes:

- Date and Time of destruction
- Method of destruction (shredded, punctured, melted)
- The Serial Number of each asset
- The Part Number of each asset
- Description of each asset

Updating the Asset Repository

Once all assets relating to a disposal have been processed by the ITAD vendor, the next step is to update the asset repository. Ensure that all assets disposed are updated to reflect their new status. Keeping a record of all disposed assets in the repository is important for any future enquires or audits. It is also beneficial to upload the certificate of disposal to the asset repository. This will show evidence of a secure disposition process, and can be used for any internal/external security audits that take place.

IT Chargeback

IT Chargeback is the process where departments are charged for the cost of assets, IT services, and software. In IT Asset Management, IT Chargeback is when the cost of an asset is directly charged to a department's cost center. This enables the IT department to recover costs directly from the organization.

An example of IT Chargeback in an organization could be when an employee requests a new computer. Since the employee works for the Legal department of the organization, once the computer has been setup and installed, the Legal department is then charged for the cost of the computer. This is a classic example of a user-based chargeback. These types of chargebacks are simple because the user is tied to only one department.

IT Chargeback can get complicated when you take into consideration assets that are not used by a single user, but rather shared between many users. Take a server running a database application for example, since the application is being used by five different departments, the server cost would then have to be evenly charged between all five of the departments. This is a common example of a shared asset chargeback.

The goal of IT Chargeback is to ensure that the cost of each asset is charged to its respective department. IT Chargeback enforces a cost saving mindset as employees and department heads are made to think carefully before submitting asset requests.

Depending on the type of organization that you are in, your organization may not have a strict cost distribution policy enforced. This means that IT Chargeback may not be possible, or needed. Introducing an IT Chargeback program requires support, financial information for all assets, and a structured process that everyone can follow. There also has to be a strong reason for wanting to implement an IT chargeback system; if your organization has no desire or need to have an IT Chargeback system put in place, then it will most likely not hold any value doing so.

By capturing and maintaining cost information in the Asset Repository, IT Chargeback can easily be applied when processing asset deployments. By integrating procurement and financial information into the Asset Repository, IT Chargeback can be processed automatically when assets are deployed for operation.

Benefits of IT Chargeback

Introducing an IT Chargeback model can benefit the organization by the following:

- Reduced IT Spend
- IT Spend Visibility
- Increased Asset Re-use
- Logical Decision Making

Total Cost of Ownership (TCO)

Total Cost of Ownership (TCO) in IT Asset Management is the total amount it costs to own a particular asset through-out its entire life-cycle. When assets are introduced into an organization, the following costs have to be evaluated:

- Asset Tracking
- IT Support
- Maintenance
- Power Consumption
- Storage

Generally when an organization purchases an asset, the actual procurement cost of the asset is only a small percentage of the total cost. Support costs can add up quickly, therefore increasing the Total Cost of Ownership (TCO) for a device.

Take a server for example, an organization may purchase a server to run a database application. The server costs $5000 to acquire. Throughout its five year lifetime, 15 incidents were opened, and a total of 110 hours were spent fixing problems that occurred with the server. Once the server reached its End of Life, the server was then put into storage, retired, and then finally disposed.

In this scenario you can see that this server occurred several financially impacting events, which contributed to the Total Cost of Ownership (TCO).

The following is a breakdown of how the Total Cost of Ownership was calculated for the server:

Expense	Cost
Acquisition	$5,000
IT Incident Support (110 hours @ $25 per hour)	$2,750
Power Consumption ($700 per year x 5 years)	$3,500
Storage	$100
Asset Tracking	$30
Disposal	$50
Total Cost of Ownership: $11,430	

As you can see from the above figures, the cost of acquiring the server was less than 50% of the actual Total Cost of Ownership (TCO). When planning for the introduction of new assets, always evaluate the potential Total Cost of Ownership (TCO), this will help the IT Help Desk forecast the support efforts for new assets.

In IT Asset Management, it is essential that the IT Help Desk associates incidents to assets within the asset repository. This will assist with tracking the total amount of time IT Engineers have worked on a particular asset. This helps the Finance and Planning Committee determine the average Total Cost of Ownership (TCO) for all types of assets.

When IT Managers and stakeholders make a decision on assets required to purchase in the acquisition stage of the

Asset Life-cycle, it is more logical to spend more money on better quality devices, and more reliable brands. In the long run, this ensures the support costs are reduced, therefore driving down the Total Cost of Ownership (TCO), as compared to buying cheaper, less reliable devices.

Similarly, to achieve cost efficiency when purchasing new assets, it's important to acquire assets that are similar to the existing devices that the organization already owns. Selecting assets that are the same brand and product series will positively contribute to all IT & technology teams. By following this method, the Total Cost of Ownership (TCO) for assets is reduced.

The following are reasons why acquiring assets of the same type will reduce the Total Cost of Ownership (TCO):

- IT Engineers won't need new training to support new assets
- Older retired assets can be stripped of their parts to be used to fix newer assets
- Incident response time is reduced due to familiarity

Return on Investment (ROI)

Return on Investment (ROI) is the term used to describe how much revenue is gained from a particular investment. In IT Asset Management, ROI is used to realize how much financial benefit an ITAM program brings to an organization.

Calculating the Return on Investment (ROI) of an IT Asset Management program can be a cumbersome and confusing procedure. One of the struggles with calculating the ROI of an ITAM program is trying to identify the amount of revenue gained, especially because no financial revenue is directly received. With that being said, an ITAM program typically saves an organization money, so savings can be calculated as revenue.

Calculating ROI

To calculate the Return on Investment (ROI), the following formula can be used:

$$ROI = \left(\frac{\text{Return from Investment} - \text{Cost of Investment}}{\text{Cost of Investment}} \right) \times 100$$

Below is an example of how the Return on Investment (ROI) can be calculated for an IT Asset Management (ITAM) program.

Investment	Formula	Annual Cost
ITAM Repository	20 users x $300 per user	$6000
IT Asset Managers	5 IT Asset Managers x $70,000	$350,000
Asset Tags	20,000 x $0.02 a tag	$400
Barcode scanners	5 scanners x $50 a scanner	$250
	Total Investment	$356,650
Return	Formula	Annual Savings
Re-use of existing assets	1500 assets a year x $500 (average asset value)	$750,000
Reduced need for IT Help Desk audits	10,000 assets x $3.00 per asset to audit	$30,000
	Total Savings	$780,000
Total Annual ROI	Savings ($780,000) - Investment ($356,650) / Investment ($356,650) x 100	118%

Benefits of calculating the Return on Investment (ROI) in IT Asset Management:

- Provides Management and Executives with a cost benefit analysis
- Continuously proves the existence of the ITAM program
- Showcases how much value the ITAM program brings to an organization
- Helps the Chief Financial Officer (CFO) recognize the cost savings realized
- Assists the justification process for additional resources

Calculating the ROI that an ITAM program brings to an organization is a great way to frequently justify the existence of an ITAM program. Depending on the granularity in your ROI calculations, defining a 100% accurate ROI calculation can be nearly impossible. Most ROI calculations can be built by using data from the Asset Repository. This is why logging every single asset transaction is important, as every time an asset is re-deployed, cost savings are achieved, and the return on investment is increased.

ITAM Maturity Model

The **IT Asset Management (ITAM)** maturity model is a model used to measure the overall success of an IT Asset Management program. For some organizations, ITAM programs are chaotic and stressful, whereas others are more proactive and disciplined. Various factors can contribute both negatively and positively to the ITAM Maturity Model of an organization. For example, running a hardware reconciliation process three days before a security audit is chaotic, whereas continuously spot checking and updating the asset repository on a regular basis is proactive.

When an organization first starts an IT Asset Management program, it's not unusual to start off as chaotic. But overtime as the program matures and grows, most organization's ITAM maturity strengthens and elevates to a more matured business practice.

Below is a table displaying the four ITAM maturity stages, including identifiable characteristics:

Stage 1: Chaotic	Stage 2: Reactive	Stage 3: Proactive	Stage 4: Optimized
No ITAM policies in place	Some assets are logged in the repository	Assets are tagged and logged in the repository	Visibility over 95% of assets within the organization
No control over any IT assets	Few processes are in place	Visibility over 60% of assets in an organization	Adheres to well defined processes and standards
No record of where assets are or who is using them	No accountability	Good communication with IT and other departments	Saves the organization vast amounts of money through asset re-use
No asset repository or discovery tool	ITAM operates in a siloed environment with little to no communication with other departments	Installs, Moves, Adds, Changes (IMACs) are frequently logged	Automated discovery tools are in place
Major security and compliance issues	Unnecessary purchases	Asset Return on Investment (ROI) can be calculated	Compliant with all security requirements and industry standards
Assets are lost and stolen with no record	No KPIs or metrics available	The asset storeroom is accurately managed	Easily demonstrate and showcase successful KPIs
Total Cost of Ownership (TCO) is unknown across all assets	Reacts last minute to security and compliance issues	Correct IT Chargebacks take place	Positive audits

As an ITAM program grows overtime, most settle at the Proactive or Optimized stage of the maturity model. Getting to the Optimized stage requires great effort over the course of many years.

Some organizations struggle to get past the chaotic stage of the ITAM maturity model, this can be caused by issues such as:

- Limited resources
- Little to no executive buy in
- No budget
- No awareness of ITAM benefits

It is also useful to remember that an IT Asset Management program is an on-going business function, and not a one-time project. Some organizations put a lot of effort into starting up an ITAM initiative, but later withdraw support. This can easily effect the ITAM maturity model, as the management and support of an ITAM program is equally as important as setting one up.

Conclusion

As the complexity of security, IT governance, standards, and technology grows day by day, the practice of IT Asset Management continuously evolves.

IT Asset Management is not something that can be mastered over night, but by implementing small changes gradually, organizations can become much more disciplined around the management of their IT assets.

By implementing the practices and processes in this book, you will be able to create a robust ITAM program that will deliver positive outcomes to any organization.

Thank You

Thank you for dedicating your time to reading this book. I hope you have enjoyed learning about the basics of IT Asset Management, and can apply the content learnt to your own ITAM projects.

Once again, thank you!

Glossary

Term	Definition
Acquisition	Acquisition is the term used to describe the process of procuring an asset.
Active RFID	Active RFID is a Radio-Frequency ID tag that utilizes the power of a battery.
Advance Exchange	Advance Exchange is the term used during an RMA when a Vendor and/or Manufacturer issues a replacement asset in advance of receiving the damaged asset.
Agent Discovery	Agent Discovery is a type of Discovery Software that installs an agent application onto each device within a network, and gathers information about the devices.
Agentless Discovery	Agentless Discovery is a type of Discovery Software that does not install software onto the devices within a network. Agentless Discovery can only detect devices that are located within a network.
Approval	Approval is the term used when a member of an organization agrees to a request.
Asset Baseline	An Asset Baseline is the term used when assets are discovered, logged, and used as the starting point for an Asset Repository.

Asset Categorization	Asset Categorization is the term used to describe the process of deciding what categories will be used for each type of asset in the Asset Repository.
Asset Check-out Form	The Asset Check-out form is an official document that is filled out when an asset is deployed.
Asset Destruction	Asset Destruction is the term used when an asset is destroyed.
Asset Destruction Certificate	An Asset Destruction Certificate is an official certificate which documents what assets were destroyed, by who, how, and when. This document is issued by IT Asset Disposition (ITAD) vendors.
Asset Downtime	Asset Downtime is the term used when an asset is faulty and/or is not working as expected.
Asset Forecast	Asset Forecast is the term used to describe the process of planning for future asset needs of an organization.
Asset Life-cycle	Asset Life-cycle is the term used that describes the different phases in which an asset goes through throughout its life.
Asset Ownership	Asset Ownership is a term used to identify the owner of an asset.
Asset Recycling	Asset Recycling is a process where recyclable parts of an asset are stripped, and re-used for future manufacturing purposes.

Asset Repository	An Asset Repository is database/software application that is used by the IT Asset Management team for the purpose of logging, tracking, and storing asset records and related information.
Asset Tag	An Asset Tag is a unique physical, alphanumeric barcoded label that is applied to hardware assets for the purpose of tracking and identification.
Asset True-up	Asset True-up is the term used to describe the process of comparing and matching asset records from a document/repository, to those that are physically present.
Audit	An Audit is the term used to describe when an internal or external organization inspects and verifies the accuracy of records.
Automation	The term used to describe an action or function that is executed by a machine reducing the need for human intervention.
Barcode	A machine-readable code in the form of vertical lines.
Best Practice	Best Practice is the term used to describe the most efficient and/or correct way of doing something.
Bill of Materials (BOM)	A Bill of Materials is a document that contains items, raw materials, and sub-components for a particular purchase.

Bill of Quantity (BOQ)	A Bill of Quantity is a document that contains items, raw materials, sub-components, and labor expenses for a particular purchase.
Budget	A Budget is the term used to describe the financial plan for a given duration of time, typically one year. Budgets typically include forecasts for the flow and distribution of cash.
Capital Expenditure (CAPEX)	Capital Expenditure is the term used to describe the amount of cash that is spent on fixed assets.
Carbon Footprint	Carbon Footprint is the term used to describe the total amount of emissions caused by an organization or asset.
Change	Change is the term used to describe a modification to the infrastructure of an organization.
Chargeback	Chargeback is the term used to describe the process of a department charging another department for the cost of IT assets and/or services.
Chassis	A Chassis is the physical structure used to house the components of a hardware device.
Chief Financial Officer (CFO)	A Chief Financial Officer is an executive member of an organization that is responsible for planning and managing all finances of a company.
Chief Information Officer (CIO)	A Chief Information Officer is an executive member of an organization

that is responsible for all Information Technology aspects of a company.

Chief Security Officer (CSO) A Chief Security Officer is an executive member of an organization that is responsible for the physical and digital security of a company.

Chief Technology Officer (CTO) A Chief Technology Officer is an executive member of an organization that is responsible for all technology and engineering aspects of a company. In most organizations the CTO and CIO are the same person.

C-Level Executive Any executive member of an organization that holds the term "Chief" in their title.

Configuration Item (CI) A Configuration Item is a configuration record that relates to an IT asset and stores its attributes and purpose.

Configuration Management Database (CMDB) The Configuration Management Database is a database that stores all of an organization's IT asset installations, also known as Configuration Items.

Consumable Consumables, also known as accessories, are assets that are not required to be tracked while in-use due to their low value, and ease of replacement.

Contract A Contract is a legal agreement between two or more organizations.

Contract Management	Contract Management is the term used to describe the process of managing contractual agreements.
Cost Benefit Analysis (CBA)	Cost Benefit Analysis is the term used to describe the process of calculating and comparing the costs and benefits of an action, project, or program.
Cost Center	A Cost Center is a department within a company where costs are allocated to.
Custodian	A person responsible for the ownership of an asset.
Data Breach	A Data Breach is the term that describes when confidential/private information is released to an unsecure environment.
Data Center	A dedicated facility that houses an organization's IT network and storage devices.
Data Destruction Report	A Data Destruction report is a report that documents the destruction of one or more assets.
Data Recovery	Data Recovery is the term used to describe when data is recovered from a defective, corrupt, or damaged device.
Data Storage	Data Storage is the term used to describe when information is stored and archived.

Database	A database is a digital application that stores information in a structured format.
Degausser	A Degausser is a piece of equipment that eliminates the magnetic field in a device, and is used for erasing data from hard disk drives.
Deployment	Deployment is the term used to describe the process of releasing an asset.
Discovery Software	Discovery Software is a type of software that is installed in an organizations network that scans, discovers, and logs assets that are connected to it.
Disposal	The term used to describe the process of removing assets from an organization.
Documentation	A set of digital or physical documents.
Donation	Donation is the term used to describe the process of giving away assets for free to another organization or individual.
End of Life (EOL)	End of Life is the term used to describe when an asset no longer holds any value to an organization.
End User Device	An End User Device is a type of asset that is specifically used by individual end users.

Enterprise Resource Planning (ERP)	Enterprise Resource Planning software is a type of application used by organizations for business process management.
Exchange	Exchange is the term used when an asset is returned to a vendor during an RMA, and is then swapped for another asset.
Executive Buy In	Executive Buy In is the term used when an executive member of an organization supports a product or project.
Finance Department	The Finance Department is a department within an organization that manages the planning, organization, and accounting for all company finances.
Framework	A set of guidelines that help individuals and/or organizations follow a specific system.
Fulfillment Request	A request that is made by an End User to the IT Help Desk for the purpose of obtaining a service or device.
General Data Protection Regulation (GDPR)	General Data Protection Regulation is a legal framework relating to the collection and processing of EU individual personal data.
Global Positioning System (GPS)	Global Positioning System is the term used to describe the space-based technology that provides the exact position of a person or object.

Hardware Asset Management (HAM)	Hardware Asset Management is the term used to describe the practices of managing hardware assets.
Human Resources (HR)	Human Resources is a department within an organization that supports the hiring, policy enforcement, and payroll within an organization.
Impact Analysis	Impact Analysis is the process when organizations analyze the pros and cons of a change to determine the outcome and impact.
Incident	An unexpected event that causes disruption to an IT service.
Information Security Management System (ISMS)	An Information Security Management System is a set of policies and procedures for managing an organizations confidential data.
Information Technology Infrastructure Library (ITIL)	Information Technology Infrastructure Library is a set of processes designed around IT Service Management. The aim of ITIL is to align IT services with the needs of an organization.
Infrastructure	Infrastructure is a term used to describe the hardware, software, or resources of an organization.
Install, Move, Add, Change (IMAC)	Install, Move, Add, Change is the term used to describe when an asset's configuration is changed in its life-cycle.
Installation	Installation is the term used to describe the process of installing an asset, or piece of software.

Insurance	Insurance is an agreement between two parties where the insurer guarantees the compensation or replacement of an asset in the case of it being lost, stolen, or destroyed.
Intangible Asset	An Intangible asset is an asset that cannot be seen or touched. Assets such as software, license agreements, and contract agreements are examples of intangible assets because they are non-physical and invisible.
Inventory	An Inventory is the term used to describe the list of IT assets electronically captured and stored.
ISO 19770	ISO 19770 is the family of international standards relating to the management of software and related IT assets. The standard primarily focuses on Software Asset Management, but also covers subjects around the management of hardware assets.
ISO 27001	ISO 27001 is an international information security standard created to support organizations with their Information Security Management System.
IT Asset	An IT Asset is a piece of information technology (hardware or software) that is used to support an organization.

IT Asset Disposition (ITAD)	IT Asset Disposition is the term used to describe the process of disposing IT assets.
IT Asset Management (ITAM)	IT Asset Management is a set of business practices implemented by an organization to track its hardware and software assets. IT Asset Management joins inventory, financial, and contractual functions into one business practice.
IT Asset Manager	An IT Asset Manager is a member of the IT Asset Management team that is responsible for managing the IT assets of an organization.
IT Governance (ITG)	IT Governance is the term used to describe the framework and policies put in place to manage the IT strategies and goals of an organization.
IT Help Desk	The IT Help Desk is a group of individuals that help the users of an organization with all IT support.
IT Service Catalog	The IT Service Catalog is a digital catalog that contains all IT services that an organization provides to its employees.
IT Service Management (ITSM)	IT Service Management is the term used to describe the process of managing the IT services of an organization to ensure that they meet the needs of a company.

ITAM Maturity Model
The ITAM Maturity Model is a model used to measure the overall success of an IT Asset Management program.

Key Performance Indicator (KPI)
A Key Performance Indicator is a measurable value that is used to measure the effectiveness of a specific business objective.

Lease
A Lease is a contractual agreement between a vendor and an organization that allows the use of specific assets for a set period of time.

Legal Department
The Legal Department is a group of employees within an organization that manage and deal with all legal matters for the organization.

MAC Address
A MAC Address is a Media Access Control Address which uniquely identifies each hardware device within a network.

Maintenance
Maintenance is the term used to describe the process of servicing and maintaining an asset throughout its life-cycle.

Manufacturer
A Manufacturer is a company that manufacturers assets and sells them to vendors and/or consumers.

Metric
A metric is a specific measure that gauges the performance of a particular activity or task.

Operating System (OS)	An Operating System is the core software application that is installed on a computer.
Operational Expenditure (OPEX)	Operational Expenditure is the term used to describe the amount of cash that is spent on supporting the day-to-day business operations.
Organization	An Organization is a hierarchy of people assigned to specific tasks within a business.
Original Equipment Manufacturer (OEM)	An Original Equipment Manufacturer is a company that manufacturers assets that may be marketed and sold by another manufacturer.
Passive RFID	A Passive RFID tag is a type of RFID tag that doesn't contain a battery, and only transmits a signal when an RFID reader is present.
PC as a Service (PCaaS)	PC as a Service is the term used to describe when manufacturers lease computers to organizations in exchange for a fixed monthly fee.
Petty Cash	Petty Cash is the term used to describe the small amount of cash funds allocated for employees to use for making immediate purchases.
Physical Warranty Card	A Physical Warranty Card is a warranty document issued by a manufacturer or vendor that documents an assets warranty.

Planning Committee	A Planning Committee is a group of employees within an organization that plan, agree, and commit to particular projects.
Point of Contact (POC)	Point of Contact is the term used to describe an individual that is approachable for information on a particular subject.
Police Report	A Police Report is an official record submitted to the police department after an illegal incident has taken place.
Policy	A set of guidelines adopted by an organization.
Problem	A Problem is the term used to describe the cause of one or more incidents.
Process	A Process is the term used to describe a set of actions that are taken to achieve an end result.
Procurement Department	The department within an organization that is responsible for procuring assets and services from vendors.
Project	A Project is a set of actions that are undertaken to make a change to a product or service.
Project Management Office (PMO)	The Project Management Office is a department within an organization that is responsible for managing the projects within a company.

Project Manager (PM)	A Project Manager is an individual that is responsible for the overall planning and delivery of a project.
Purchase Order (PO)	A Purchase Order is a document issued to a vendor from a buyer, which lists out all of the assets that the buyer wishes to purchase.
Purchase Requisition (PR)	A Purchase Requisition is an internal request that is sent to the procurement department of an organization to request the procurement of new assets.
Rack	A Rack is a physical structure that is used for housing the computing equipment of a data center.
Radio-frequency Identification (RFID)	Radio-frequency Identification is a type of wireless technology that transmits data via radio waves through an electronic chip.
Random Access Memory (RAM)	Random Access Memory is a type of data storage used within computers that is used for storing temporary data.
Reconciliation	Reconciliation is the process where two sets of records are compared against each other to validate the accuracy of the inventory.
Redeployment	Asset Redeployment is the activity when existing assets are returned, and then later re-deployed for operation.

Repurposing	Repurposing is the term used to describe when an asset is re-used for another purpose.
Request for Information (RFI)	Request for Information is a process in which organizations gather information about vendors to determine which one may be the best fit for the purchase of new services or assets.
Request for Proposal (RFP)	Request for Proposal is a document that is sent out to existing or potential vendors for the purpose of procuring new assets or services. An RFP document is an invitation to vendors to participate in the selection process for a new business proposal.
Request for Quote (RFQ)	A Request for Quote is a business process in which organizations invite suppliers/vendors to submit bids for new services or assets.
Requestor	A Requestor is an individual who has made a request.
Responsible, Accountable, Consulted, Informed (RACI)	A RACI is a matrix chart used for documenting and identifying the roles and responsibilities of a process or project.
Retirement	Retirement is the term used to describe when an asset is removed from operation.
Return Authorization (RA)	Return Authorization is the term used to describe when an asset is returned back to a vendor.

Return Goods Authorization (RGA)	Return Goods Authorization is the term used to describe when an asset is returned back to a vendor.
Return Merchandize Authorization (RMA)	Return Merchandize Authorization is the process that happens when a faulty asset is returned to a manufacturer or supplier to be repaired, replaced, or refunded.
Return on Investment (ROI)	Return on Investment is the term used to describe the amount of revenue that is gained from a particular investment.
Return to Vendor (RTV)	Return to Vendor is the term used to describe when an asset is returned back to a vendor.
Security Operations Center (SOC)	Security Operations Center is a team within an organization that continuously monitors and analyzes the security of an organization.
Security Risk	A situation or action that poses a risk to an organization.
Security Team	A Security Team is a group of Information Security professionals within an organization that protect the data and network of an organization from unauthorized access and misuse.
Self-service	Self-service is the term used to describe the model of allowing users to access a service themselves without the need of assistance.

Serial Number	A Serial Number is a manufacturer issued identification number used for identifying a particular asset.
Service Asset and Configuration Management (SACM)	Service Asset and Configuration Management is the term used to describe the activities and processes defined by ITIL around managing configuration items within an organization.
Service Level Agreement (SLA)	A Service Level Agreement is a contract agreement between a service provider and a client that defines the level of service that will be delivered by the service provider.
Shipping Courier	A Shipping Courier is a company that manages the transportation of packages and freight for their customers.
Shredding	Shredding is the term used to describe when an asset is destroyed using a shredder.
Software as a Service (SaaS)	Software as a Service is a term commonly used in the IT industry that describes a software application that is hosted in the cloud by a software vendor. User access is gained to the application via the internet, enabling users to use the software anywhere, and at any time.
Software Asset Management (SAM)	Software Asset Management is the term used to describe the business practices of managing the software an organization owns and uses.

Software License	A Software License is a legal agreement that authorizes the use of a software application.
Spreadsheet	A Spreadsheet is a digital document that stores data in columns and rows.
Stakeholder	A Stakeholder is a member of an organization that has interest or is involved in a project.
Stock Keeping Unit (SKU)	Stock Keeping Unit is an identification number that is assigned to products and services for the tracking and management of them.
Storage	Storage is the term used to describe when an asset is not in use, and is kept in a storeroom.
Storeroom	A Storeroom is a dedicated location where hardware assets are securely stored.
Support Agreement	A Support Agreement is a contractual service support agreement between a vendor and an organization.
Tangible Asset	A Tangible Asset is an asset that has physical properties.
Tax Saving	Tax Saving is the term used to describe when an organization saves money through fixed asset depreciation.
Technology Refresh	Technology Refresh is the term used to describe when an organization replaces current assets with new assets.

Terms and Conditions	Terms and Conditions are rules put in place as part of a contractual agreement.
Total Cost of Ownership (TCO)	Total Cost of Ownership is the total amount it costs to own a particular asset through-out its entire life-cycle.
Tracking	Tracking is the term used to describe the process of managing and logging an asset's information throughout its life-cycle.
Tracking Number	A Tracking Number is a unique number issued by shipping couriers for the purpose of tracking shipments.
Universal Serial Bus (USB)	A Universal Serial Bus is a common device interface that allows computer devices to connect with each other.
Vending Machine	A Vending Machine is a self-service machine that allows users to instantly obtain products.
Vendor	A Vendor is a company that sells assets and/or services to organizations.
Vendor Agreement	A Vendor Agreement is a legal agreement between a vendor and an organization.
Vendor Management	Vendor Management is the term used to describe the activities around managing the vendor's an organization procures assets and/or services from.

Vendor Scorecard   A document used to log and track the performance of a vendor.

Warranty   A warranty is a contract agreement between a manufacturer, and an organization that promises the repair or replacement of an asset when it becomes damaged.

Warranty Label   A physical label that is applied to hardware assets to indicate an available warranty.

Wiping Data   Wiping Data is the term used to describe the process of removing data from a hardware device, and making the data unreadable.

Workstation   A workstation is a term used to describe a desktop computer.